DGE
OOKS

Marvelous MONEY TRICKS

by Norm Barnhart

CAPSTONE PRESS
a capstone imprint

Edge Books are published by Capstone Press,
1710 Roe Crest Drive, North Mankato, Minnesota 56003
www.capstonepub.com

Library of Congress Cataloging-in-Publication Data
Barnhart, Norm.
Marvelous money tricks / by Norm Barnhart.
pages cm.—(Edge books. magic manuals)
Includes bibliographical references.
Summary: "Step-by-step instructions and photos show how to do a variety of fun
and entertaining tricks using money"—Provided by publisher.
ISBN 978-1-4765-0134-5 (library binding)
ISBN 978-1-4765-3390-2 (ebook PDF)
1. Coin tricks—Juvenile literature. I. Title.
GV1559.B373 2014
793.8—dc23   2013004920

Editorial Credits
Aaron Sautter, editor; Tracy Davies McCabe, designer; Svetlana Zhurkin,
media researcher; Jennifer Walker, production specialist; Sarah Schuette,
photo stylist; Marcy Morin, photo scheduler

Photo Credits
All interior photos by Capstone Studio/Karon Dubke.
Cover and background images by Shutterstock/Angela Waye, Anna Subbotina,
Dmitri Melnik, Liliya Kulianionak, serg_dibrova, and temastadnyk.

Printed in the United States of America in Stevens Point, Wisconsin.
032013   007227WZF13

TABLE OF CONTENTS

Amazing Money Magic

If a magician asks to borrow a dollar bill, get ready to be amazed! Magicians love performing incredible tricks for big crowds. But they don't need a huge stage or fancy props to amaze an audience. Magicians can entertain people with simple tricks using only a few coins or dollar bills.

In this book, you'll learn to make nickels appear to change into dimes. You'll make coins appear to transport from one place to another. You'll even make dollar bills seem to appear out of thin air. Practice the tricks on the following pages and get ready to astound people with marvelous money magic!

MONEY MAGIC SECRET: SECRET POCKETS

Magicians often hide objects in secret pockets for their tricks. These pockets are often hidden inside ordinary objects. Below are some secret pockets used for tricks in this book. Always handle objects with secret pockets as if there were nothing special about them. Handling things casually will help keep the audience from guessing the secrets to your tricks.

Handkerchief:
Sew a secret pocket into the corner of a handkerchief to hide a coin.

Box:
Use extra cardboard to make a secret pocket in a box.

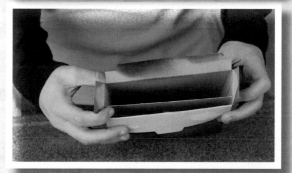

Newspaper:
Glue two pages of a newspaper together to form a secret pocket inside.

LeaPing Lincoln

It's a race to the top as these two presidents battle it out. Your friends won't believe it when Abe Lincoln instantly leaps ahead of George Washington!

What You Need:
- a $1 bill
- a $5 bill

PERFORMANCE:

1. Show the audience the two bills. Ask a volunteer to look at the money to make sure the bills are normal. Then place the money on the table with the $1 bill on top as shown. Say, "Did you know that Abe Lincoln was once a wrestler? Whenever he wrestles George Washington, he usually comes out on top."

2. Roll up the bills. As you begin, point to the $1 bill and say, "Notice that George starts out on top."

3. Once the bills are rolled up, casually let the top corner of the $5 bill flip over the top. As you do this, hold the corner of the $1 bill snugly with the roll. This simple move puts the $5 bill on top. Do this smoothly so the volunteer doesn't see the secret to the trick.

4. Now say something like "Mighty leaping Lincoln!" Then unroll the bills to show that the $5 bill is now on top.

TIP: Try asking someone in the audience if you can borrow some money for this trick. People are always amazed when their own belongings are used to perform incredible magic.

LUCKY LEPRECHAUN

Leprechauns are imaginary creatures that hide treasure at the end of rainbows. Your friends will be astounded when they see coins magically rain from a paper rainbow into the leprechaun's kettle.

What You Need:

- one sheet of paper
- one large photo of a rainbow
- several coins
- a decorative bowl
- glue

PREPARATION:

1. Glue the photo of the rainbow onto the sheet of paper to create a secret pocket. Leave one corner unglued by the end of the rainbow.

2. When the glue is dry, slide the coins into the pocket.

PERFORMANCE:

1. Take out the decorative bowl and show it to the audience. Tell them, "I usually don't believe in stories about leprechauns, gold, and rainbows. But then someone gave me this little pot and told me it once belonged to a leprechaun."

2. Show the picture of the rainbow to the audience. Pinch the secret pocket closed with your thumb and finger to hold the coins in place. Tell the crowd, "I wonder if we can fill this pot with some leprechaun treasure?"

3. Place the bowl on the table in front of you. Then roll up the picture of the rainbow into a tube. Keep the secret pocket closed until you are ready for the coins to drop out.

4. Hold the tube over the bowl, and then take a deep breath and blow through it. As you blow, release the pocket so the coins rain down into the bowl.

5. Pick up the bowl full of coins and stare at it in surprise. Then look at the audience and say, "Well, it's not a pot of gold, but it looks like we found the leprechaun's secret treasure!"

TRICK THREE
A FiSt FULL OF DOLLarS

This trick is very popular with audiences. People are stunned when you make a handful of bills appear out of thin air!

What You Need:
- several money bills
- a long-sleeved shirt or jacket

PREPARATION:

1. Roll the bills into a tight roll.

2. Hide the roll of bills by tucking it inside a crease of one sleeve near your elbow.

PERFORMANCE:

1. Smile and tell the audience, "I don't like to keep my money in a wallet. I'm afraid it will get stolen. Instead, I like to keep my cash in an invisible magical safe."

2. Begin rolling up your sleeves. Start with the sleeve that is not hiding the roll of bills. As you do this, hold out your other hand to show the audience you aren't hiding anything in it.

3. Next, roll up the sleeve that is hiding the roll of bills. Hold out your other hand to show the audience you aren't hiding anything there either. As you roll up the second sleeve, secretly grab the hidden roll of bills and hide it in the palm of your hand.

4. Now bring your hands together. Give the audience a smile and begin rubbing your hands in a magical way. Use your thumbs to gently unroll the bills.

5. Unroll the bills completely and hold them up to show the audience. Or you can let the bills rain down one at a time. It will look like the money magically appeared out of thin air! Tell the audience, "This is a great way to keep my money safe. I don't even need a bank!"

TIP: Practice this trick in front of a mirror until you can do it smoothly and casually. You don't want the audience to see you grab the secret roll of bills from your shirt sleeve.

Mysterious Vanishing Coin

The plot thickens with this trick! It's a mystery when a coin vanishes from a volunteer's hand. But all will be revealed on the last page of a mysterious book.

What You Need:
- three identical coins
- two identical handkerchiefs
- an old book
- a table
- a magic wand
- scissors
- needle and thread

PREPARATION:

1. Cut one corner off one handkerchief large enough to cover one of the coins.

2. Place the corner piece on the matching corner of the second handkerchief. Sew the pieces together to form a secret pocket. Place one of the coins in the secret pocket before sewing the last side shut.

3. Place a second coin inside the old book on the last page.

PERFORMANCE:

1. Take out the old book and show it to the audience. Then place it on the table. Tell the audience, "This is one of my favorite mystery stories. It's about a greedy magician who uses magic to steal coins. But with mystery stories, there's usually a surprise on the last page."

2. Take out the handkerchief and the third coin. Show the coin and hanky to the audience and say, "The magician used a simple handkerchief to hide his money."

3. Pretend to cover the third coin with the handkerchief (3a). As you do this, secretly drop the coin into the palm of your hand to hide it (3b). At the same time, grab the secret hidden coin and bring it to the middle of the hanky. It will look like you are holding the coin inside the handkerchief.

4. With the coin hidden in your hand, reach into your magic case to get your magic wand. Secretly drop the hidden coin into the case as you pick up the wand.

5. Now ask a volunteer from the audience, "Could you please hold the coin inside the handkerchief? Something mysterious is about to happen." Have the person hold the coin inside the handkerchief.

6. Wave the magic wand over the handkerchief in the volunteer's hand.

7. Quickly pull away the handkerchief to show that the coin has vanished! This will amaze the volunteer because he or she can feel the coin until the last moment.

8. Ask, "Where do you think the coin went? Just open the book to the last page and the mystery will be solved!" When the volunteer finds the coin ask him or her to hold it up and show the audience. Take a bow as they cheer your mysterious magical ability!

DOUBLE your money

Want to double your money in a flash? With this incredible trick you'll be turning nickels into dimes in the blink of an eye!

What You Need:
- a nickel
- a dime
- a playing card
- clear double-sided tape

PREPARATION:

1. Place a piece of double-sided tape on the center of the playing card.

PERFORMANCE:

1. When you're ready to do this trick, reach into your magic case for the coins and playing card. With your hands hidden from the audience, place the dime in your palm and then cover it with the nickel. Hold the card with your other hand.

2. Hold out the nickel to show the audience. Say, "Do you ever wish you could double your money? I discovered an easy way to turn nickels into dimes."

TIP: Keep the audience's attention focused on the dime by focusing on it yourself. Directing an audience's attention in this way is a useful method magicians often use in their shows.

3. Set the card down on the nickel in your hand. Position the card so the secret tape sits on the nickel. Gently press the card down so the tape sticks to the nickel.

4. Get out your magic wand and hand it to a volunteer. Have the volunteer wave the wand over the card and say some magical words like, "Duo Double Doubloons!"

5. Lift up the card to show that a dime now sits in your hand. Hand the dime to the volunteer and ask him or her to show it to the audience. As the volunteer does this, casually drop the card with the nickel into your magic case. Tell the crowd, "This is the fastest way I know to double my money. Unfortunately, it only works with nickels."

The Vanishing President

U.S. presidents have a very stressful job. They like to get away for a vacation sometimes. With this fun trick, you can help send a president on a tropical getaway.

What You Need:

- a postcard showing the U.S. White House
- a postcard of a tropical location
- two identical coins
- a small cloth mat
- glue

PREPARATION:

1. Glue one of the coins face-up to the top of the White House postcard.

TIP: Magicians often use a small mat called a close-up mat. The mat acts like a little stage to help focus the audience's attention on the trick. It also allows coins to be set down quietly to avoid giving away a trick's secret.

PERFORMANCE:

1. Place the mat on the table in front of you. Then take out the tropical postcard and the second coin. Keep the coin hidden behind the postcard with your thumb (1a). Show the postcard to the audience. Say, "This is my favorite vacation spot. It's a really beautiful place." Then set the postcard on the mat with the coin secretly hidden under it (1b).

2. Next bring out the postcard with the first coin glued to it. Tilt the card up so the audience can see the coin. But be careful not to turn it too much. Don't let the crowd see that the coin is stuck to the postcard. Tell the audience, "Presidents are under a lot of stress. They deserve to go on a nice vacation. Let's see if we can send this president on a special tropical vacation."

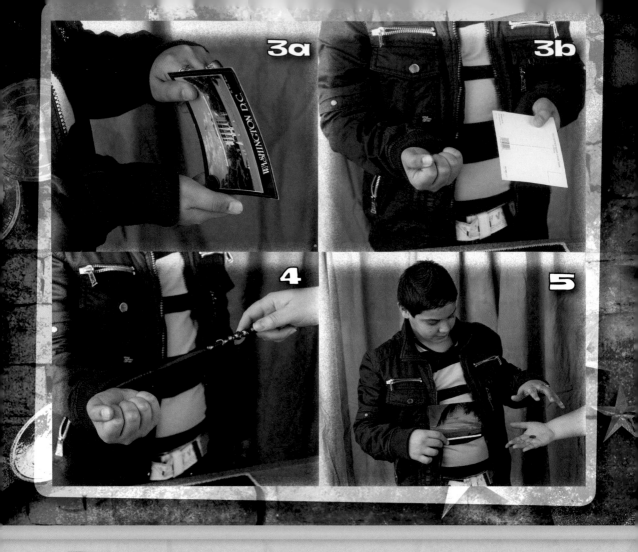

3. Next, tip the postcard toward you to make it look as if you're dumping the coin into your hand (3a). Close your hand and hold it up to look like you're holding the coin (3b). Keep the postcard turned upside down. Casually place it in your magic case as you grab your magic wand.

4. Ask for a volunteer to help you with the next step. Tell the audience, "Watch closely as we send the president from my hand to the beautiful beach." Have the volunteer tap your hand with the wand. Then open your hand slowly. The audience will be surprised to see that the coin has disappeared!

5. Ask the volunteer to turn over the tropical postcard. Then ask the person to pick up the coin and show it to the audience. Say, "I sure hope the president enjoyed his tropical vacation!"

COUPON CASH-IN

Need cash fast? With a little magic, you can turn coupons into instant cash money. All your friends will want to learn this incredible trick to get rich quick!

What You Need:

- a sheet of newspaper
- several coupons cut about the size of dollar bills
- five $1 or $5 bills
- glue

PREPARATION:

1. Fold the sheet of newspaper in half to make two layers.

2. Glue the sheet of paper together to form two separate secret pockets. Make the pockets slightly larger than the coupons and money bills.

3. Hide the money bills inside one of the secret pockets.

PERFORMANCE:

1. Bring out the sheet of newspaper and show both sides to the audience. Say, "Using newspaper coupons is a great way to save money. But sometimes I just don't have time to go to the store to use them."

2. Roll the newspaper into a cone. Take out the coupons and show them to the audience. Say, "I found a much faster way to turn my coupons into cash!"

3. Slide the coupons into the second secret pocket inside the newspaper. Practice this move ahead of time until you can do it smoothly.

TIP: Practice this trick in front of a mirror so you can see what it looks like to the audience.

4. Now wave your magic wand over the newspaper and say a few magic words like, "Presto, change-O!"

5. Look into the cone, and then give the audience a big smile. Reach into the cone and pull out the secret hidden bills. Hold them up to show the audience.

6. Let the newspaper fall open to show the audience that it is empty, and then put it away. Give the audience a big smile as you count the cash. Tell them, "This magic business sure saves me a lot of time and money!"

Big Surprise Prize

Everyone loves a fun surprise! Your friends will be stunned when they see a pile of coins pouring out of a popcorn box.

What You Need:
- a popcorn snack box
- thin cardboard
- 30 coins
- a bowl

PREPARATION:

1. Empty the popcorn from the box. Measure the width and height of the popcorn box. Cut the thin cardboard to match these measurements.

2. Slide the piece of cardboard into the popcorn box to make a secret pocket.

3. Place the coins into the secret pocket. Place some popcorn back into the main part of the box.

TIP: Try preparing several of these boxes ahead of time with different prizes. Then ask some volunteers to wave the magic wand. People will have fun thinking they made the prizes appear.

PERFORMANCE:

1. Show the popcorn box to the audience. Tell them, "Popcorn is my favorite snack. But what I really love is the prize at the bottom!"

2. Pour the popcorn into a bowl. As you do this, use your finger to hold the secret pocket closed so the coins don't fall out. The audience will think it's a normal box and that it is now empty.

3. Look into the empty box and say, "Hmm, I don't see the prize. I might need to use some magic to find it." Wave your magic wand over the box and say a magic word like, "Alakazam!"

4. Tip the box over and allow the coins to drop into your hand. Tell the audience, "What a great prize! I got my favorite snack—and my money back too!"

TRICK NINE
Pirate's Treasure

Could pirates use magic to hide their treasure? They could if they knew this trick! The audience won't believe their eyes when several coins suddenly appear in an empty treasure chest.

What You Need:
- a small felt-lined box, such as a jewelry box
- two identical hankerchiefs
- needle and thread
- 10 coins

PREPARATION:

1. Sew the two handkerchiefs together along the outside edges. Leave a 2-inch (5-centimeter) space open at one corner.

2. Sort the 10 coins into two stacks of five. Place both stacks in the jewelry box. Then place the box inside your magic case.

TIP: This trick can be changed for almost any kind of story you want to tell Instead of a pirate story, try telling the audience that you found a new way to hide money from your brother.

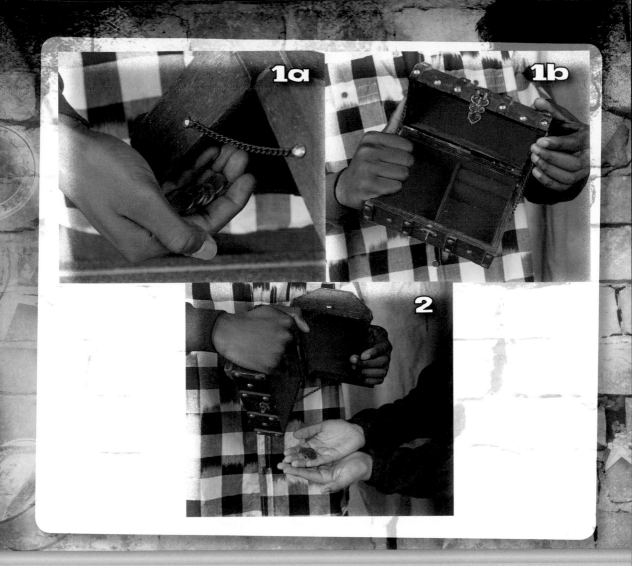

PERFORMANCE:

1. Reach into your magic case to take out the jewelry box. As you pick it up, hide one stack of coins against the side of the box with your fingers as shown. Hold up the box to show the audience and say, "I found this small chest in an old antique shop. The shopkeeper said it was a magical treasure chest once owned by an old pirate."

2. Ask for a volunteer to help with this trick. Tip the chest over and dump the five loose coins into the person's hand. Be sure to keep the other five coins hidden by your fingers against the inside of the box. Then say, "The chest came with five coins. Would you please count them?" As the volunteer counts the coins, set the box on the table. Let the hidden coins drop down inside the box and close the cover.

3. Now pick up the handkerchief and casually slip one finger into the secret opening (3a). Use your other hand to bring up the other corners of the handkerchief to form a small sack (3b).

4. Take a few steps away from the jewelry box and ask the volunteer to join you. Say, "We're about to see something amazing! Please hand me the coins one at a time and count each one out loud." As you take the coins from the volunteer, place them into the secret pocket in the handkerchief. Use a smooth motion so it looks like you are simply dropping them into the middle of the sack.

5. Now pick up your magic wand and say, "According to the legend, the pirate used a magic wand to make his treasure fly into the treasure chest." Wave the wand over the sack and then point it at the jewelry box. Do this once for each coin.

6. Pinch the secret opening shut with your thumb and finger. Then quickly snap the handkerchief open to show that the coins have disappeared! Then say, "Let's see if the coins traveled to the pirate's treasure chest."

7. Pick up the jewelry box and have the volunteer hold out his or her hands. Then pour the coins inside the box into the volunteer's hands. Ask him or her to count the coins out loud for the audience. People will be stunned to see that the coins all traveled magically through the air!

READ MORE

Einhorn, Nicholas. *Alakazam! Sensational Magic Tricks with Silk, Thimbles, Paper, and Money.* Inside Magic. New York: Rosen Central, 2013.

Fullman, Joe. *Coin and Rope Tricks.* Magic Handbook. Buffalo, N.Y.: Firefly Books, 2009.

Lane, Mike. *Coin Magic.* Miraculous Magic Tricks. New York: Windmill Books, 2012.

INTERNET SITES

FactHound offers a safe, fun way to find Internet sites related to this book. All of the sites on FactHound have been researched by our staff.

Here's all you do:

Visit *www.facthound.com*

Type in this code: 9781476501345

Super-cool stuff! Check out projects, games and lots more at **www.capstonekids.com**